SIX DEGREES
TO
YOUR DREAMS

SIX DEGREES
TO
YOUR DREAMS

Laura Handke Jones

iUniverse, Inc.
New York Lincoln Shanghai

Six Degrees to Your Dreams

iUniverse books may be ordered through booksellers or by contacting:

iUniverse
2021 Pine Lake Road, Suite 100
Lincoln, NE 68512
www.iuniverse.com
1-800-Authors (1-800-288-4677)

ISBN-13: 978-0-595-36193-9 (pbk)
ISBN-13: 978-0-595-80640-9 (ebk)
ISBN-10: 0-595-36193-5 (pbk)
ISBN-10: 0-595-80640-6 (ebk)

Printed in the United States of America

CONTENTS

INTRODUCTION VII

WISHWEAVERS SONG XI

THE SIX CONCEPTS: XIII

PART ONE: MOVING FROM DREAMS TO GOALS 1

    CONCEPT ONE: BEING GENTLE WITH YOURSELF
        (AND OTHERS) 3

    CONCEPT TWO: LISTENING TO YOUR INNER
        VOICE/INTUITIVE NATURE (IVIN) 13

PART TWO: MAKING IT REAL 21

    CONCEPT THREE: KNOWING WHAT YOU WANT 23

    CONCEPT FOUR: ASKING FOR HELP 29

PART THREE: LIVING WITH THE REALITY 35

    CONCEPT FIVE: BEING PREPARED 37

    CONCEPT SIX: OVERCOMING ROADBLOCKS 43

CONCLUSION 49

ACKNOWLEDGEMENTS 51

RESOURCE DIRECTORY 55

A TRIBUTE TO GRANDMA HANDKE 59

INTRODUCTION

Your life is about to change.

Picking up this book is a pivotal moment for you.

My life changed in 1999 when I helped create a women's group that was begun for the "soul" purpose of helping each other realize our dreams and goals. The concepts and practices we used were so simple and so successful, and I became so impassioned about sharing them with others, my business—Wishweavers—was born. Becoming involved in the women's group, which was named M to the Sixth Power (M^6 for short), was a pivotal moment for me—a choice which changed the direction of my future.

The process is as simple as taking a step and allowing the magic to happen.

We named the group M to the Sixth Power, or M^6, because M refers to the realm of mystical magic, movement, motion and more practically, master minding principles. The number 6 refers to the six people who were in attendance at that first meeting, along with the six degrees of separation theory, which I call the six degrees of connection. Within no more than six steps from you is the person, resource, connection you need to accomplish your dream. I'll be describing how in the following pages, and here are a couple of concrete examples from my own life.

Just a few months after the creation of M^6, I walked into one Thursday evening meeting with a wild dream. I was so jazzed about the concepts we'd been using and how successful they'd been, so passionate about sharing them with other people, I voiced my dream to create a videotape to send to Oprah Winfrey. Judy, one of the other M^6 members, looked at me with an expression on her face I will never forget. I could almost see the lightbulb over her head. She said her big dream had been to bring many people together in one room, all helping each other create their dreams. This idea had come to Judy months before, and she'd jotted some notes down, then misplaced them.

Judy, Patty (another M[6] member) and I decided to get together the following week in my kitchen and map out a plan for making the big workshop, and the video for Oprah, happen simultaneously. At the very next M[6] meeting a woman named Julie showed up for the first time because she had heard about our group on the local cable access channel, CCTV. AJ, program host, had come to a few meetings and interviewed the group on her TV show, *Tapestry*. Julie knew how to operate a professional camera, and had the equipment. She was so excited about the video, she invited Joni to the next meeting. Joni had experience with editing and had been wanting to get back into film production work. About the same time, I had read an article about someone I used to work with in the insurance business; Don's passion was also camera and video work. Judy found the notes she had tucked away and forgotten about. Then, a friend I hadn't seen in over two years, Ginger, visited over New Years Eve and knew someone who knew someone who had just been hired on by Harpo Productions as a field producer.

Once I voiced my video dream, all the pieces started falling into place. The first key pieces within less than a month. Until September 11, 2001, when the whole world shifted focus, I had every reason to believe these concepts would be featured on Oprah's show. I knew exactly the day the pitch had been made to the top producers.

I admit the outcome wasn't what I had hoped at the time. The Wishweavers workshop was not featured on Oprah's show, nor did I receive a call expressing interest or asking for further information. Yet, looking back, I see a different perspective and amazement in the connections leading to the Oprah video and a specific Harpo Productions employee. Oprah's program was frequently about "living the dream" at the time, and after September 11, 2001, the focus of her shows quickly shifted.

Wishweavers wasn't my business at the time—it was still in the dream stages. My book hadn't yet been written. Perhaps I wasn't ready for an international audience just then.

Perhaps because you are reading this book right now, and I am sharing my experience, new connections will be formed for both of us to realize our dreams, so we can help other people accomplish theirs.

When you take one step towards your dream, you'll be greeted with a hundred other possibilities in return. I agree with what Oprah says, "I believe that you are here to become more of yourself and live your best life." We are meant to follow our dreams, to be happy, successful and joyful. This is something I don't just believe, I *know*.

Last summer I made a trip to South Dakota, where I was born and raised, to spend time with my family and some college friends. My parents' farm is an hour drive from Watertown, so I typically book plane tickets to fly into the airport there. Because I had plans to see college friends, including staying two nights with Lori at her horse ranch near Sioux Falls, I flew into Sioux Falls instead of Watertown.

At the Minneapolis/St. Paul, Minnesota airport (the stop between Oregon and South Dakota) I noticed a woman with a book, clipboard, papers and pen sitting in the waiting area. I remember thinking to myself, "She must be either a teacher or a writer." For some reason, I felt drawn to her. I noticed her travel bag with jungle animals printed on the fabric.

The same woman was seated next to me on the flight from Minneapolis/St. Paul to Sioux Falls. We were both tired on the plane, dozing and didn't say anything to one another for quite some time.

Finally, she turned to me and asked, "Are we there yet?"

I had been sleeping and didn't know, looked out the window and said, "I don't think we've left yet."

We both cracked up. We hadn't even taken off. We introduced ourselves, discovered we'd left Portland on the same flight, and during that short plane ride, a friendship was formed. Kathie was indeed a teacher and a writer (weight management was a current topic); she was also an editor.

In just the one year since we first met, I've completed my book proposal draft and Kathie has edited it for me. We both love to walk for exercise. We've talked theatre and acting at length and have double dated with our husbands for dinner and a play. Kathie has directed 21 plays and is a wonderful actor, loving the acting process as much as I do. I've taken photos of her which are nearly as fine as those done by a professional photographer. Kathie now offers weight management classes under the Wishweavers umbrella for people whose dream is to lose weight and keep it off; she's one of the Wishweavers resident experts. I've helped her with her brochure.

These are the kinds of connections which will happen for you when you begin traveling the road to your dreams. All you need to do is take a step and pay attention. It's truly that simple. In the following chapters, I'll describe how to pay attention and how to further the six degrees process.

My paternal grandmother, Norma Handke, passed in 1999—the same year M^6 was born. One of the many valuable treasures I was given after her death was her journal entries from 1962 to 1994. In 1994 she stopped writing, after her memory had left her and she was simply surviving day to day. I wish I had been able to share some of these concepts with her.

What I read in my beloved grandmother's journals, years after she had written them, surprised me. She was always so good to me and I loved her deeply. Grandma was one of my idols, a woman who was orphaned early in life and not only put herself through college while working for her board and room, but also sent help to her younger sister in foster care. Until I read her journals, I wasn't aware of the disparaging thoughts she had about herself, or how many unfulfilled dreams she took with her to the grave. Excerpts from the journals begin each of the six concepts in this book.

I dedicate this book to the loving spirit of Norma Amelia Hahn Handke (August 11, 1910—September 1, 1999), or as I always called her—Grandma Handke. Grandma, thank you for all the love and joy you shared with me. You're in my heart, always.

WISHWEAVERS SONG

Music and Lyrics by Jenny Limbaugh

I was thinking about my future,
I was dreaming of what I could do,
and I was thinking maybe I'm crazy,
but I took the chance and I called you.

You heard my story, you thought about it
and said you had an idea or two,
and I had this feeling all of a sudden
that I had the power to make it come true!

I brought a vision, you brought connection,
together we build a road to a dream.
We have the power, we create the future.
Believe in your vision and follow your dream.

Weave your wishes with the wishes of others
and soon you have woven a fine tapestry.
Somebody else has just what you needed—
come hear my story because maybe it's me
and maybe it's you who has something for me!

I brought a vision, you brought connection,
together we build a road to a dream.
We have the power, we create the future.
Believe in your vision and follow your dream.
Believe in your spirit and follow your dream.
Believe in your wisdom and follow your dream!

THE SIX CONCEPTS:

- Being Gentle With Yourself (and Others)
- Listening to Your Inner Voice/Intuitive Nature (IVIN)
- Knowing What You Want
- Asking For Help
- Being Prepared
- Overcoming Roadblocks

PART *ONE*

MOVING FROM DREAMS TO GOALS

CONCEPT *One*

Being Gentle With Yourself (and Others)

Can't help envying her some. It must be really thrilling to stay in a lovely place, go out for every meal, and feel you look like a million instead of a fat cow like me. Seems like the specter of inferiority rears its ugly head every so often. Somehow this trailering bit has lost its thrill for me. It's the first time, except when Lee was sick, that I've just yearned to be home. Marth never even mentioned the Christmas gifts. Baked bread and a crock pot of beans.
—January 11, 1979

*W*hen I tell people my job is to bring people together with the other people, resources and talents they need to realize their dreams and goals, I often hear something like, "How can you help me make a million dollars?"

There's nothing wrong with wanting to have a million dollars in the bank. Or to be the President of the United States, or the Prime Minister of England. Or a movie star, or a hermit living in the woods, writing poetry. We all have dreams and the power to create the kind of life we want to live.

I like to ask people why they want a million dollars. People's desires and dreams stem from the feelings behind those dreams, the emotions they wish to experience on a regular basis. Each individual's personal history and vision determines why they want what they want, and how it's best for them to go about getting it.

One person may want a million dollars in the bank because she has a burning desire to start her own non-profit foundation, while another may have the same dream because he's exhausted from scrambling to pay the bills and put food on the table. The former may have been raised in a wealthy, yet stingy, family environment and knows her purpose is to feed the hungry children around the globe. The latter may have been raised by a single parent with six siblings and no opportunity for educational advancement. He knows he wants the security, independence and freedom a million dollars would bring.

Same dream. Different motivations. Both want to do something positive for themselves and the people they care about. These two would-be millionaires would be well served knowing the same three things:

- Why they want the money

Personal history and emotions are huge factors, perhaps the hugest, in people understanding why they want what they want.

- How they are going to get it

This is where the six degrees come in. Do these people know how to connect with those who can help them, and those they can help?

- What they are going to do with it when they have it

If the vision is clear ahead of time, it will be much easier to know what to do with a million dollars when it starts rolling in, a hundred dollars at a time.

I would ask both would-be millionaires the same two questions:

1. Are you passionate enough to make a million dollars and passionate enough to pursue your dream?

The journey is even more important than the destination. Working at a job you hate in order to make a million dollars is going to leave you emotionally, physically, spiritually and mentally bereft, making your chances of putting a million dollars in the bank less likely than your chances of ending up in the hospital.

If you need to temporarily work at a job to pursue your dream, make sure the job is in alignment with your inner integrity, and you know it is short term. Have your financial goals and time frame written down and stick to the plan. The clearer your long term vision is, the better you'll be able to choose a job which puts food on the table and pays the bills while you're making steps to accomplish your goal. Pay very close attention to the people you meet in these jobs. You will feel a connection with some and not others. Chances are, those you feel a connection with will come to greet you, and you them, later down the road when you're more fully living your dream. That's certainly been the case for me.

Every job will give you valuable contacts and skills; you have a choice whether to focus on the positive or negative aspects of the job. If you come home complaining about your job or your co-workers every night, you want to either remove yourself from the environment and find a new job, or examine your own thought processes. What is your emotional pay-off for staying there?

I worked in banks for three and a half years, then with an insurance company for nearly seven. After years of becoming depressed on Sunday evenings and coming home drained five days a week, I finally realized: a) neither of those industries were a good match for me, and b) I did have other options. Yet I met some amazing people and learned valuable skills in both banking and insurance. My background in developing classes and training people in the workplace began because of two generous and encouraging supervisors I was blessed to work with at the insurance company. Both helped germinate seeds of potential I didn't realize I possessed at the time.

I remember one adjuster trainee I mentored. Lisa was extremely bright, articulate and had exceptional writing skills. As time went on, it became clear she was poorly matched for the job of a claims adjuster. She was always overwhelmed, behind and frustrated. Lisa was devastated upon losing her job during a reduction in force. Yet it was only after being released from that particular job she started pursuing her passion. I resigned during that same reduction in force because the policies of the company no longer aligned with my inner integrity. Last I heard, Lisa had become an elementary school teacher and was finding the true fulfillment in her work she never found in the insurance world.

Sometimes we need a kick, a boost, to get us out of a bad situation we're not seeing for ourselves so new doors can open. We tend to lean towards perceived security (a steady paycheck, health and retirement benefits) instead of our own hearts. The truth is there is no such thing as security. In this economic climate, people who've put money into retirement funds for many years lose those funds every day. The only certainty is change. The only sure way to manage that change is to listen to your heart and realize your own dreams.

I don't regret my years in the insurance business, although I probably could have resigned about two years earlier. I didn't because of that perceived security. The experience and feedback I received as a claims mentor and trainer were priceless when I struck out on my own and eventually founded Wishweavers. That's when my passion truly kicked in. It takes persistence, patience and tenacity to launch a dream like my dream of helping other people with their dreams on a large scale. If your dream is to make a million dollars, but you're not passionate about whatever it is you're doing to get there, you'll become discouraged at the first setback or fork in the road. Passion is what keeps the dream alive and growing, one small step, and some huge leaps, at a time.

2. Do you have a plan and know the people to help you get there?

None of us work or live in a void. The hermit writing poetry in the woods by the lake works with the deer, trees, earth, air and water. The person starting a burgeoning business works with clients and vendors. The single mother connects with other mothers to swap day care arrangements and plan birthday parties for the kids with decorations and cakes. None of this is small stuff; it's all meaningful. It's about connecting.

In concept four you'll learn how to easily create your own Wishweavers circle. The people in your circle will help you form the plan and help you get there within six degrees, while you are doing the same for them.

Okay, so you want a million dollars. Are you paying attention to your own finances right now? Do you know about saving and investing and how emotional bank accounts relate to money? Are you energetically attracting or repelling money? What is your emotional history with money? With the help of someone in my circle, I'm learning about emotional money awareness, residual income, making my money work for me rather than me working for my money, taking educated financial risks and discovering what is truly an asset verses a liability.

So you want to be a hermit in the woods writing poetry by a lake. Do you know people who live in the areas you have envisioned for yourself? If no people live there, do you know the property? Can you see it clearly in your mind's eye? I met a mortgage broker and real estate agent in my first circle. Is there a possibility someone you know might know someone who knows someone who rents a cabin every summer just a mile down the road, or in a state within a day's drive? When you form your circle, you jump start the six degrees into action so you can find those connections for yourself and for others.

If your vision, your dream, is clear, you will know someone who knows someone who will lead you towards your dream, and you to theirs. If your vision, your dream, is unclear, you will find the people to help you solidify it. Now it's up to you to be kind and gentle with yourself and others while you're in the process of making your dreams real.

Being kind and gentle begins with communication.

Have you ever listened to the way you talk to yourself? I mean really listen. Start by doing one thing: pay attention to your thoughts. You might want to shut this book right now, go about your daily activities, and monitor your thoughts for one full hour. It's helpful to keep a notebook with you and jot those thoughts down.

What did you learn about the way you talk to yourself? Personally, I was shocked the first time I did this exercise, and I did it for an entire day. I had no idea the ongoing dialog inside my head was so critical of other people. I remember driving down Commercial Street thinking to myself, "Why on earth is that woman walking down the sidewalk wearing those awful stretch tangerine colored pants? They look terrible on her!"

Even more shocking were the critical thoughts I was having about myself. Much like with my grandmother's journals, which I hadn't read yet at the time, I found I was filled with thoughts of inadequacy and fearfulness. I was blaming myself for possibly being late, having a bad hair day, wondering what I did wrong that made the man in the green car honk, feeling inadequate and fearful about my next meeting and ability to pay a bill. In truth, I wasn't late, and even if I had been it wouldn't have truly mattered, nor would have my hair. I had nothing to do with the man in the green car honking; it wasn't about me at all. Once I got there, the meeting was fine, and somehow I was able to pay the bill.

In my work helping myself and others manifest our dreams into reality since 1999, I have found our thoughts about ourselves and each other are the first place to start. We can choose to let our random thoughts create drama in our lives or we can choose to change our thoughts.

How often do we say to ourselves, "I can't", "I must", "I should", "I shouldn't"? And how often have those internal words made us feel better about ourselves, more able to accomplish our dreams and reach for the stars? How often have using those same words with others altered their behavior or made the relationship stronger in the long run? I'd say right about zero percent of the time. Pay attention to your thoughts and the way you talk to yourself and others. If you don't like what you're hearing, alter it by consciously changing your thoughts. Your life will start to change as a result and you'll be tapping into those six degrees before you know it.

Following are two short exercises you can use to move into this first concept of being gentle with yourself while you're in the process of creating your dreams and making some positive changes in your life. None of the exercises in this book are time consuming, and all will help you reach your goal destination, or clarify what that is for you, much more quickly. If you cannot do them all at this time, choose one or two and stick with your choices daily for several weeks. You will begin to see yourself becoming more positive, calm and more willing to believe you can achieve your dreams and goals.

IF YOU DON'T HAVE AN INSPIRATIONAL QUOTE COLLECTION, FIND OR CREATE ONE

I start off every morning by reading an inspirational quote from a daily calendar a friend gave me as a holiday gift last year. Prior to that, every morning I read the daily quote from a perpetual calendar a friend and colleague published. Patricia was in the M[6] group and we helped her when she decided she was going to form a publishing company and publish her own calendar. I've loved words for as long as I can remember and have been collecting quotes since my high school days. I keep those which are positive in nature, and many are thought provoking. What speaks to you? Certain verses from the Bible? Your favorite writer? Buddhist traditions? A favorite poem? I went so far as to stencil *The Road Not Taken* by Robert Frost on the wall by the window in my inspiration room, which also serves as my office space when I work from home.

What you turn your attention to first thing in the morning sets your tone for the entire day. Why not start your day on a positive tone? I can't tell you how many times I've awakened with a concern on my mind, and turning to some uplifting words to remind me how powerful and loved I am helped completely turn my mood around. Why not give yourself the same gift? Why not use this as a tool to help yourself and others tap into the six degrees? When a quote is meaningful to me, it's often meaningful to others. When a phrase sings to me, I put it into my quarterly newsletter. Often, when I'm meeting with someone with a dream, one phrase or another will come back to me so I can share it with them and they can share it with others, furthering the six degrees.

> *"Would you tell me, please, which way I ought to go from here?" asked Alice.*
> *"That depends a good deal on where you want to get to," said the cat.*
> —Lewis Carroll from Alice's Adventures in Wonderland

KEEP A RUNNING JOURNAL OF YOUR THOUGHTS AND FEELINGS

I write three pages in the morning as Julia Cameron suggests in *the Artist's Way*. Cameron calls it morning pages; I call it a mind dump. When I clear the clutter in my mind by dumping it out on paper (I have a little tendonitis in my right hand, so I usually use a computer) the mind clutter stops coming back to haunt me. Release, let go, and move ahead with your day. You can set your goal for fifteen minutes per day. You don't have to write three pages, if that feels daunting to you. You can write twenty pages, if you find it helpful. Just be regular about it, in whatever manner works best for you. These pages are meant for your eyes only. If you share them with others, you may censor yourself. Your writing wants to be safe from prying eyes.

Wait a few weeks before you review your pages and look for common, repeating themes, such as when you are being hard on yourself. Simply look for those recurring themes, and find a positive thought with which to replace the negative one. This takes only a few seconds.

You may notice, "I'll never have the money to go to France." Going to France is a dream, a goal! Replace the negative thought with, "I have one dollar to start my France fund today." Get out an envelope, label it France and put a dollar in it. Or a quarter, or even a penny. Or a quick sketch that looks like how you see a plane ticket to France looking, a magazine clipping of the Eiffel Tower.

You may notice, "I'm so fat." Replace it with a characteristic you like about yourself. Losing weight is a dream, a goal! If you honestly can't think of one positive characteristic about you in that moment, pick up the phone and call a friend you trust to be nonjudgmental and supportive, and ask the friend what positive trait she first notices when you walk into a room. "I'm so fat" has now become "I have a beautiful, brilliant smile." You internalize this as you tell it to yourself, over and over.

You just started changing your thoughts. Congratulations! Keep recording those new thoughts and feelings. What you write will change along with your new thoughts about yourself and others. If you write consistently, you'll find steps of the six degrees starting to show up in your pages. Once you've acknowledged it's a dream to go to France, you'll start paying more attention to the people you meet who may be able to help you get there. An exceptional travel agent may be recommended by a new acquaintance. Someone may know someone who has tickets to Paris and wants to unload them quickly and cheaply because they can't make the trip. Someone you've known for a long time, who didn't know you were looking for additional income until you mentioned your dream to go to France, may recommend a source of residual income in the form of a great real estate deal.

As you pay attention to your own dreams, you'll naturally start paying attention to the dreams of others to help them jump start the six degrees as well. Perhaps after you find your friend has a dream of losing weight, you will run across a pertinent article to clip for him in your favorite magazine, or someone wanting to exchange their health club membership for six months of child care after school, something your friend is willing and able to do.

Just keep on replacing your negative thoughts with positives ones, writing consistently and paying attention to the links you begin to find. Enjoy the new life you're consciously creating for yourself and others as it unfolds even further into the six degrees towards your dreams.

> *The significant business of your life is alive and well, awaiting discovery, within your very soul. You and I were born to come into ourselves as complete and distinct persons. Accepting this, we build a valuable life.*
> —Marsha Sinetar

> *A man may fall many times but he won't be a failure until he says someone pushed him.*
> —Elmer G. Letterman

Overview of Concept One:

- Know your underlying motivations

- Passion is critical

- Formulate a plan

- Find people to help you

- Be kind to yourself

- Pay attention to your thoughts and make them positive

- Keep inspirational quotes

- Journal and watch for trends

CONCEPT *Two*

Listening to Your Inner Voice/Intuitive Nature (IVIN)

Started to clean bedroom but somehow I've lost my starch. I just have to get hold of myself. I know this is right but I love this place so—it's foolish—I feel I have to store memories. There's less than two months left. I must get hold of myself for I don't want the kids to feel bad. When the house gets out and I can see where our new home will be then surely I won't have this awful empty feeling.

—July 26, 1968

*E*veryone has what I call an Inner Voice/Intuitive Nature or IVIN. Some might call the IVIN that little voice in the back of my head, some a gut feeling, some women's intuition, some God. Whatever you want to call it, it's there. I've found the IVIN to be my best friend in finding the six degrees to my dreams. Have you ever been driving somewhere with the directions written down or printed from the internet, and a feeling told you to turn left instead of right at a particular intersection in spite of the directions? Or that if you went around the block, you'd find a parking space? That's your IVIN at work.

The following example is a good illustration. Prior to launching my Wishweavers business, I worked one day a week to supplement income at a lovely gift and antique shop close to my home. I was the only person in the store one day when a young man walked in. He seemed cagey, excitable, and the hairs on my body stood on end in his presence. He stayed in the store looking haphazardly around at things until all the other customers in the store had left. He then engaged me in conversation. A voice inside my head seemed to scream, "He's going to steal your purse!" He spoke mostly in monolog about a number of things, and I became more and more uncomfortable with each word he said.

Finally, he said he wanted to buy an antique kerosene lamp to ship to his grandmother who collected them on the east coast, and asked me if we had a box in which to ship it. I later learned this is one of the oldest tricks in the book for stealing from a retail store. I hesitated for a moment before going into the back room, that voice still in my head. I looked down at my purse behind the counter, made direct eye contact with the man, and left the purse there rather than taking it with me into the back, not wanting to offend him should he turn out to be a legitimate paying customer.

I'd never moved as hastily as I did grabbing that box. The man was standing by the front door as I came out, easily less than three seconds later. He said, "I need to go to my car to get my wallet," walked out the door and bolted down the sidewalk. I quickly glanced behind the counter. My purse was still there, but when I looked inside it, my billfold was missing. I raced out the door and he was already long gone.

I searched, notified the owners of the other businesses in the strip mall, called the police, filed a report—the usual things people do when they've been robbed. The man had left a plastic soda pop bottle on the counter, which was dusted for fingerprints to no avail. My billfold was later found in a hobby shop not far from the store, completely intact except for the one dollar bill and change I had in it. The billfold was also dusted for fingerprints and none were found on it, either.

The message from my IVIN was absolutely clear, yet I didn't heed it out of fear of offending someone. I learned a big lesson that day. Listen to your IVIN! It won't lead you astray, even if you can't always interpret the message right away. I didn't even need to interpret that one; the words and accompanying feelings which came were so strong, I simply knew this person's intention was to steal from me. Not that he had a gun and was going to demand I empty the cash register to rob the store, but that he intended to steal from me personally.

Our IVIN helps us realize our dreams just like it alerts us to potential danger. Another philosophy I live by is what I sometimes call the Three Time Rule. We receive little nudges, often unbeknownst to us, meant to bring us another step closer to realizing our dreams and creative potential. I'm thinking back now to a day in college towards the end of my senior year. I majored in broadcast journalism my freshman year at South Dakota State University. One of my classes entailed an assignment doing radio spots and editing (at that time, literally splicing) the tape with a partner. My partner's name was Marilyn. Marilyn and I had the best time doing that assignment, laughing our way through most of it. As you can imagine, we had to tape over and over again because of the laughter, so we were in the studio the entire afternoon. I don't remember what kind of a grade I got on that assignment, but I do remember the fun Marilyn and I had together.

I switched majors to psychology and eventually sociology after that term and didn't see Marilyn again for three years. Then in the last few days of my senior year, I ran into her three times in three different locations in one day. We were both astounded. Had I known then what I know now, I would have invited Marilyn for a cup of coffee—or more likely, at the time, a beer. This Three Time Rule philosophy has proven itself to me over and over. If I see or read about something more than just a couple of times, I look into it and virtually always find some gem of inspiration I needed to move another degree or two closer to my dreams. Sometimes three different people will recommend the same book to me within a short period of time, and reading that book gives me an entirely new perspective, an alternative route to accomplishing my dreams I hadn't seen before.

The IVIN can work in mysterious ways. Our task is to simply pay attention and take action. I went to see the movie *Stepmom* starring Julia Roberts and Susan Sarandon in the theater with a friend. It was not just entertaining, but enlightening to me, as I married a man with three half-grown boys from his first marriage, so am a stepmom myself. Months after I'd seen the movie in the theater, it was on TV several times. I found myself watching parts of it three different times within a period of about two weeks. After the third time, I picked up the phone and called the boys' natural mother and invited her to lunch. I had met Laurie—we all live in the same town—yet had never gotten to know her.

That first lunch was the start of a friendship. The friendship led to improved communication during the challenging periods which inevitably come about in a blended family situation, any family situation. The improved communication and friendship brought me another step closer to my dreams. Laurie worked for the school district and was able to provide me with information I wouldn't otherwise have had access to for an educational workshop offered under the Wishweavers umbrella targeting school age children. My husband's ex-wife was one of the six degrees to my dreams.

The key to tapping into your IVIN is simply to pay attention and take a step. Then pay more attention and take another step. Here are ways you can tap into your IVIN to bring you even closer to utilizing the six degrees to accomplishing your dreams.

FIND QUIET TIME FOR YOURSELF EVERY DAY

When your mind is filled with clutter, you won't hear your IVIN. I've found this step to be one of the easiest, and at the same time most difficult, practices to incorporate into my daily life. We have a tendency to go, go, go and do, do, do when we're in the process of creating our dreams. It's easy to get so caught up in the going and doing we don't take the time to listen to what our IVIN has to say until we crash from exhaustion or come up against a road block. Then we don't have a choice but to listen. Then, it's easy!

Listen and pay attention first, before you hit the road block. One way to do this is to take daily time for prayerful meditation and deep breathing. All meditation means is becoming quiet and emptying the mind of thoughts, observing the thoughts while they come in without judging them, then watching them go. This is the best way I know of to open up to guidance from the IVIN.

I heard Dr. Michael Abrams, author of *The Twelve Conditions of a Miracle*, speak in Wilsonville, Oregon earlier this year. From his presentation I learned more about the pre-frontal lobe in the brain. Studies have been done on the brain in people who meditate and people who don't. The pre-frontal lobe, the intuitive area of the brain, is like any muscle—when exercised, more blood flows there. If a person meditates for just fifteen minutes, the results remain in the entire body for hours, sometimes up to a day later. The heart beat slows, breathing is more relaxed, and body and mind are more at peace.

Meditation causes increased blood flow to the pre-frontal lobe and less to the frontal lobe, which is the area of the brain (a very large area, while the pre-frontal lobe is very small) reserved for fight and flight responses, what Dr. Abrams calls the lizard of the brain. That's the area which causes us to react to things in panic or preservation mode and gets us into a worrying funk. Meditation and deep breathing calm those knee-jerk responses and help us pay attention to the IVIN, our best friend in linking with the six degrees to our dreams.

You don't have to sit in a dark room with a candle or incense burning to meditate. Meditation can be accomplished during a 15-30 minute walk in nature. I regularly meditate while walking, when I want to combine prayer with exercise. Seeing the lush green of the trees against the vivid blue of the sky, while hearing the cheerful sounds of birds and insects and feeling the ground under our feet can lead to immediate appreciation of natural beauty—therefore less thoughts—allowing us to more naturally tap into the IVIN.

> *Don't underestimate your inner voice. It rarely speaks to you as the cartoons portray it—a devil on one shoulder and an angel on the other. That would be easy. In reality, our inner voice is usually very quiet. It gets drowned out by the noise of life or ignored in the rush. But it will take care of you, guide, help you. Listen.*
> —Moments for Myself, a calendar by Blessings Unlimited

DO SOMETHING CREATIVE OR DIFFERENTLY

This suggestion relates to the brain as well—get those left and right brain sides working together! My client, friend and colleague, Lucy, recommends writing with both your dominant and non-dominant writing hands, trading off, when checking in about where to go with your dreams, finding that next link in the six degrees. If you're right handed, writing with the left hand as well (even though the script may be more difficult to read!) kicks the other side of your brain into action, so the two can work together.

Dry off after showering or bathing in a different way in the morning. If you usually towel your hair first, dry your feet first this time. Your back tomorrow. As I'm writing this section, I'm sitting at a table on the sidewalk with a notebook and pen in front of a coffee house, while I usually write on the computer in my inspiration room and home office.

Take a different route to a regular destination. Pay attention to what you see on the different route. Your sixth degree could be found simply because you decided to take Red Leaf Avenue to the grocery store instead of Main Street. One of the people I've interviewed, who is living her dream (the owner of the gift and antique shop I mentioned earlier), found her graphic designer while she was driving and a large pencil sculpture in front of the artist's studio caught her eye. She knew the designer thought like she did, and the rest is a dream come true, a wonderful step within the six degrees connection.

Do you have any magazines or catalogs stacked up to take in for recycling? Pull them out, go through the pages, and rip out every image, word, phrase and detail which sing to your IVIN. This is one of the most time consuming practices I recommend—it could take several hours. It's also one of the most fun and sometimes the most surprising. I created a collage with my images on a cork board with push pins I already had. One of my clients used a plastic cover, which looked like the lid of a box. Another made something more like a portfolio. No matter how you decide to create the collage, it's an effective tool and will help you learn more about your dreams and the six steps to getting there.

In my own collage, with only a few magazines and catalogs on hand, I found a number of surprises. I love to cook and eat homemade food, yet was surprised when pictures of pasta sauce, herbs and cheese ended up in my collage. It reminded me how important it is to nurture my body, spend time in the garden, and create delicious and healthy food for myself and others, when I want to. I only cook when I feel like it, and the more I nurture my dreams, the more I feel like it! Our bodies need to be healthy to carry us forward while we're working on the six degrees to our dreams.

I'm a white woman, raised in the heart of the U.S. My collage was filled with people of different races and ethnic backgrounds. This reminded me of the importance of diversity, and to actively seek out that diversity, when I'm missing it in day-to-day life. Diversity and new thoughts, ideas and backgrounds are all keys to the six degrees to my dreams, as they are to yours. Take the opportunity to do something differently, something creative, something fun, and see where those steps lead you.

When the deepest part of you becomes engaged in what you are doing, when what you do serves both yourself and others, when you do not tire within but seek the sweet satisfaction of your life and your work, you are doing what you were meant to be doing.
—Gary Zukav

<u>Overview of Concept Two:</u>

- Pay attention to your inner voice and gut feelings

- Embrace silence and solitude daily

- Breathe!

- Be creative, do different things, and do things differently

PART TWO

MAKING IT REAL

CONCEPT *Three*

Knowing What You Want

I am having an awful time with me. Have been unable to throw off my disappointment at not going to Alaska and to Martha's. Why can't I just accept the fact it's work, work and more work, that's The Thing. I keep myself unhappy all the time!

—June 8, 1970

Tuesday and now a year later we leave for Alaska! Went by way of Jamestown and got out to beach and had supper with Thelens, Pam and Glenn and had a nice evening.

—June 8, 1971

T hese two exercises are the best way I know of to discover what it is you truly want, if you don't know already, and if you already do, to further solidify it. The six degrees are kicking in all the time, and the more finely tuned your wish is, the more closely and quickly you'll be able to align with those six degrees.

In concept one, we explored how people's individual backgrounds determine why they want what they want and how it's best for them to go about getting it. That doesn't mean we are slaves to our histories, however. The phrase "Today is the first day of the rest of your life" may be a cliché, yet it's still true. Life starts all over again in each and every moment. As Dr. Wayne Dyer says in *10 Secrets for Success and Inner*

Peace, give up your personal history. You don't want the wake behind the boat to drive the boat. Then all you do is go in circles.

You're leaving the wake behind when you do the **ME NOW**™ exercise. Do it in writing and see it clearly in your mind's eye. Everything in this exercise is targeted for precisely who you want to be in the ME NOW that is truly you. If you are $50,000 in debt and struggling to pay bills working at a job you hate now, you are debt free and have $100,000 invested in the ME NOW. If you are living in the suburbs and really want a farm with livestock, you're living on that farm in the ME NOW. The key is to know who you want to be as if you are that person now. Then you will become that person. It's important to **Visualize, Journalize, Vocalize**™ your dreams to connect with the six degrees. I'll talk more about that in a bit.

ME NOW

Imagine your life, yourself, as a clean slate, a newborn, in the sense you have left preconceived images and ideas of yourself behind. This is the ME you truly are within and are about to become in daily life, using the six degrees of connection to help you.

Wake up in the morning and notice your surroundings. What are the colors, textures, scents, sounds and beings—people, animals, plants, etc.—around you? Did you wake up in a king size bed with a rich thread count in the sheets, on a bed of pine needles in the forest, in your very own house boat? Wherever you start is your ME NOW.

Read your daily inspirational quote and go to the bathroom. Look in the mirror. Look very closely. Who do you see? Who is this person? What do you look like? Why is that sense of joy and peace in your eyes? What have you done with your life to come to this point?

Where do you go from the bathroom? What are you wearing? What do your surroundings look like? Again, what beings are around you? What do you smell? What do you eat for breakfast?

This exercise is a lot of fun. Just take yourself step by step throughout a twenty-four hour period, a week if you wish, noticing how you're feeling and what you're sensing. I'm making a presumption you want to be a happy person, so that's what you saw in the mirror. If you want to be an unhappy person, I can't help you. What I'm asking you to do is look at that happy person in the mirror and know why ME NOW is happy. Use your IVIN to guide you.

What gifts, talents, skills and energy are you using to better your life and the lives of others? Where does this energy come from?! Why is there such joy in the daily life of ME NOW? Write down every single detail. Know your contribution to the world and where your money comes from, what you are doing with your time and resources.

You'll break the steps down with the help of your Wishweavers circle. For now, let your imagination run wild.

I completed a similar exercise called Your Ideal Day, from the book *Wishcraft*, by Barbara Sher with Annie Gottlieb, the first time in the fall of 1999, just after M^6 was formed. All the critical pieces in that particular ideal day manifested into my life within six months. Of course, it was no coincidence the real estate agent and mortgage broker who helped my husband and I secure our dream property out of town were both in M^6.

For example, in your ME NOW, you may be working as a free-lance consultant from your home office. Your home is well organized and a greyhound dog is your canine companion. You might start off like this:

I awaken to golden sunlight streaming through my bedroom window at 6:45 am. I do not own an alarm clock because I awaken every morning well rested, eager to begin the day. I recently redecorated my bedroom and the room is imbued with warm red and gold hues, filling me with a sense of luxurious richness. A brilliant white lilac bush blooms outside my bedroom window. I stretch luxuriously as does my dog and pal, Jeremy. My body is flexible, fit and healthy. I slide from between the creamy sheets and place my bare feet on the smooth wooden floor beneath my shaker style bed. A precious rug at the foot of the bed was designed and created by my neighbor in the earth-friendly community I have chosen to live in. As I walk to the hand-hewn side table to read my daily inspirational quote, I feel at peace with the world and my contribution to it. A smile rests on my face as I…

The key is to focus on whatever details are important to you and what you are _feeling_. Once you start, you likely will not want to stop. Let the inspirations and images come, without censoring yourself in any way. This is a powerful step to meeting that first degree to your dreams.

VISUALIZE, JOURNALIZE, VOCALIZE

Visualize, Journalize, Vocalize™ is a phrase I created to verbalize what I know to be true. Bringing your dreams and wishes to light and into reality using the six degrees of connection is a three part process. This process uses different learning styles for those who are visual, auditory or tactile. You see what you want, and deserve, clearly in your mind's eye. If you can't see it yourself, how are you going to go about describing it to others and getting it? You write it down because that makes it real and helps solidify details and concrete goals you may be missing. And you share it with others, vocalizing, which kicks the six degrees of connection into action.

In concept four you'll learn how to create your own Wishweavers circle. I recommend, before forming your circle, you complete the ME NOW exercise, and know going in which one to three critical pieces to your ME NOW, your dream, you want to work on first.

Let's go back to the example above. You might want to first focus on how you can use your skills, abilities, talents and gifts as a consultant, and brainstorm with the group how to best create and implement the business package only you can offer. Or get feedback on how to organize your home, how to find a greyhound dog, or all three. No matter which dreams you choose to share, someone will have an idea, a contact, a resource for you, as you will for them. Your neighbor's brother could know someone spearheading an organization devoted to finding good homes for retired racing dogs. Someone may have just seen such an organization featured at your local PetsMart. A woman responding to a flyer you posted might want to start a business called Clemma's Bodacious Clutter Busting, because organizing is one of her greatest gifts and skills. The person she invites may be a successful consultant locally, wanting to expand business to the national or international level.

Being prepared will help you to be an example for others, and you'll also be one degree closer to bringing your own dreams into reality.

> *The future belongs to those who believe*
> *in the beauty of their dreams.*
> —Eleanor Roosevelt

<u>Overview of Concept Three:</u>

- Complete your ME NOW exercise with feeling

- Visualize, Journalize, Vocalize

- Prepare to be an inspiration and example to others

- Get ready to form your own Wishweavers circle and create your dreams!

CONCEPT *Four*

Asking For Help

Pam came over and scrubbed the kitchen and utility for me. Boy how that helps!! Got beds made and just as we were eating supper Marth called from Watertown. O my, such excitement. They got here around 8:00.

—October 16, 1981

*F*or many people, asking for help is the hardest part. When I started my first business, a home-based match-making service, marketing was the hardest part for me. I hated doing flyers, placing ads and asking people to do business with me. It felt inauthentic.

I've learned a few things since then. The match-making service wasn't really my dream, my purpose. The opportunity came into my life because I was meant to end my career in the insurance industry, get to know the owner of the global match-making company, learn to be self-employed and meet some incredible people along the way. Matching people with their dreams and the resources, talents and other people needed to accomplish them was a better fit for me than matching people with romantic partners. I needed some help to make the transition and learned what help truly meant.

Let me make this very clear. **You are not asking for help. You are offering to help.** When you create and realize your dream and fulfill your purpose, you are giving the gift of yourself to other people. No one else has what you have to offer, only you do. Your unique talents and

.ts, like the irises of your eyes or the prints on your finger tips, cannot /e duplicated. They belong to you and you alone.

When you form a Wishweavers circle, you are giving of yourself. While you are receiving the inspiration and resources you need to create your dreams, you are also giving the same back to everyone who comes into your circle. It's a win-win situation; there are no losers in this kind of co-creative environment.

Starting out is very simple. Just pay attention to the people in, and coming into, your life. How do you feel about them? What do the conversations entail? Listen to your IVIN—it will tell you which people to invite into your circle, whether they are friends or family members you've known for years or someone you met at a bus stop yesterday. When you're comfortable with what your IVIN is telling you, make a list of the people you know with a dream and contact them. Only two or three people are needed to form an initial group, and the cost is nothing more than something to write on and something to write with.

Set a specific time and place to meet. It could be at someone's home, a coffee shop or restaurant, library, meeting hall—anywhere with enough quiet for focus. You can place an ad in the paper or post flyers inviting fellow Wishweavers, whatever feels best to your heart. If you have an internet mailing list, use it!

Set a time limit, for example two hours, and come prepared to take notes and absorb any resources you receive. There is merit in every idea—this isn't the place to debate what may or may not work. Consider how often you're going to meet—once a week, twice a month, monthly?

Divide the time equally by the number of people in attendance. Use a timer! Some will need more, some less—time is allotted equally and those with less time can pass their time onto others. Share what you want to achieve, or what you need help with. If some individual dreams are vague, others help make the steps more concrete.

At the end of the meeting, narrow down and focus. It's helpful to write down the next three steps in chronological order. Individual commitments are encouraged at the end of the meeting. For example, "I commit that by our next meeting I have drawn up a brochure draft and researched website domain names." Or, "By the fifth of next month, I have uncluttered the junk closet in the garage." Being accountable to the group provides motivation and support.

You may want to create any or all of the following:

- Wishweaving Group flyer
- Basic Guidelines sheet for new members with a brief bio of each current member
- Mission Statement

Ex: Empower people to define and realize their dreams and goals. Embrace individual diversity and contributions with an emphasis on creativity in areas of interest. Give directions to dreams with encouragement and practical support.

Consider keeping a notebook or folder with business cards and information on each person. Carry it with you in case you run across someone or some thing which will help another achieve their goal/dream.

As the group becomes larger, generally more than a dozen or so, break off into smaller groups. Maintain a general member list and consider convening with the entire group quarterly or bi-annually in a larger Wishweavers experience format.

It truly is that simple. As you're changing your thoughts about yourself and others, paying more attention to your IVIN, you will naturally draw to you the people to help you realize your dreams, and you theirs. Remember, you are not asking for help. You're offering to help.

Keep the following principles in mind:

SEVEN MASTER MIND PRINCIPLES

I RELEASE myself to the Master Mind because I am strong when
I have others to help me.

I BELIEVE the combined intelligence of the Master Mind creates a
wisdom far beyond my own.

I UNDERSTAND that I will more easily create positive results in my
life when I am open to looking at myself and my problems and opportunities from another's point of view.

I DECIDE to release my desire totally in trust to the Master Mind and
I am open to accepting new possibilities.

I FORGIVE myself for mistakes I have made. I also forgive others who
have hurt me in the past so I can move into the future with a clean
slate.

I ASK the Master Mind to hear what I really want; my goals, my dreams
and my desires, and I hear my Mastermind partners support me in my
fulfillment.

I ACCEPT—I know, relax and accept; believing that the working power
of the Master Mind will respond to my every need. I am grateful knowing this is so.

Here is some sample verbiage you can use for written materials or a verbal introduction:

Congratulations on taking a step toward making your dreams come true, and to helping others weave their wishes!

Wishweavers operates from the philosophy that within no more than six degrees from you are the people, resources, ideas and support to help you make your deepest wishes and most heartfelt desires a reality. Someone knows someone, who knows someone, who knows someone who has what you need to make your dreams come true. You have the ideas, resources and know the people to help others weave their wishes as well.

Six degrees of connection means everyone on Earth can be connected using six associations or less. Reflect for a moment on what this truly means. Six associations or less. This is powerful. You are—at most—no more than six steps away from accomplishing whatever goal you want to accomplish, achieving whatever dream you want to achieve.

A Wishweavers experience is directed, interactive and participatory. All people in attendance have the opportunity to discover, clarify, define and affirm their dreams and wishes—and share resources, information, contacts and strategies with others. Each participant walks out with a design, a treasure map, in place.

Each individual's contribution is cherished and important. We help each other align with our most heartfelt wishes and give each other the tools to create the reality of our dreams. It's no coincidence you're reading this. There's a reason you were drawn to it. Someone is dreaming you into their life right now so you can help them weave a wish, and someone is out there just waiting to hand you the key to unlocking the life of your dreams. Simply by taking the first step, you're changing universal energy in incredibly positive ways.

Congratulations. Welcome to your dream.

<u>Overview of Concept Four:</u>

- Asking for help is actually offering to help
- Pay attention to the people in your life and choose other dreamers
- A Wishweavers circle can be formed with only two or three people
- Set a date, time and place and invite people!
- Divide time equally among attendees and use a timer
- Apply Master Mind principles
- Write down next steps, make commitments and meet regularly

PART *THREE*

LIVING WITH THE REALITY

CONCEPT *Five*

Being Prepared

Still seems like a dream. We all went down to depot together. What a ride over & thru the mountains. The train just seemed to hang on the side of the mountain. What scenery! I wondered how the gold seekers ever got through and the poor horses & the railroad builders. Decided we'd just stay in a parking lot & so we did & O, how it rained.
—June 23, 1971

*H*ere you are. You've taken the first steps towards your dreams. How does it feel? Exhilarating? Scary? Both? Guess what? That's normal.

Remember one thing, if nothing else, throughout this process. Only share your dreams with people who will support and buoy you with encouragement. I mentioned this in the portion about daily journaling. Your personal writing and dreams want to be shared only with people who will help you move forward and past perceived obstacles. There is no place for negativity, drama or nay-saying during this process. We tend to create enough of this in our own mind without help from others! This is why you've created your Wishweavers circle, with those of like minds. You will help each other move past roadblocks and understand where, how and why you may be stuck. Cutting down each other's dreams is not a part of the process. This was the message of the keynote speaker at the very first Wishweavers workshop in October, 2000. Patricia entitled her speech, *Anchoring Your Dreams*.

As you move into your new reality with the dreams you've been nurturing and nourishing, people you've known for years may not recognize the YOU NOW. A certain he may feel threatened. A certain she may feel left behind. Close friends or family members may have lost their security blanket in the YOU THEN. If you already have half your France fund saved, are looking into travel arrangements, and your husband hasn't saved a dime, he may wonder if you're going without him. This could lead to an argument if you let it. If you've lost eight pounds and your sister has gained ten, she may feel resentful and unsure of herself, which may again lead to a disagreement if you let it.

Don't let it.

Your Wishweavers circle is where you turn to discuss your dreams, segues and next steps. With the husband, the sister, wife, parent, child—whomever it is who may feel threatened or left out—here are three completely cost-free steps to take in that moment an argument or disagreement may occur, before you turn to your WW circle for onward, forward momentum.

PERSONAL EXPANSION GOALS

You want to know where you're going, what your intention is for your own life, before you can interact with others in the spirit of the six degrees of connection between us all. This is true of those who are on the same path, and those who are not. Otherwise you'll react from a place of uncertainty or defensiveness and allow other people's reactions or perceptions to color your own responses.

Your Personal Expansion Goal (PEG—reminding you you're climbing your adventure one peg at a time) can start by being as simple as: I am a conduit of inspiration and good, helping bring abundance into my life and the lives of others.

If you choose to fine tune it, your PEG may become something like:

I facilitate real estate transactions, purchasing and renovating properties in foreclosure. I provide affordable housing for low income families while adding to my own prosperity.

I'm a teacher with a wealth of information to share. I provide valuable inspiration to students eager to learn. I change students' lives one class at a time, while adding to my financial abundance. My published book provides residual income.

I'm a full-time mom because being a parent is the most awesome job on this planet. There is no bigger blessing or responsibility than raising the spirits and souls of children in human bodies to better the future of our planet. Because I have invested well and wisely, our financial needs are met, and I have plenty to give back and circulate.

Write your PEG down and allow it to change and grow as you change and grow. Post it somewhere you will see it daily and keep it with you in your wallet or billfold. If something someone else says brings up doubt, frustration or anger in you, repeat your PEG to yourself silently. Feel free to share aloud your PEG, parts of it, or an altered version, with the person. Or you can simply say, knowing YOU know your PEG, "This is the path I've chosen and I'm very happy with the choices I've made."

LISTEN

There are many books available on the power of listening and artful communication. This isn't one of them! It's important to touch on listening in the context of this concept, however. Very often people who come across as negative simply want what they feel is best for you. They don't want you to be hurt if you fail. They most likely haven't read Wayne Dyer's *10 Secrets for Success and Inner Peace* and learned about the myth of failure. As Dyer says, there is no such thing as failure. Everything we do simply produces a result.

If you make a chocolate soufflé and it falls the first time, do you whine and cry about being a failure as a chocolate soufflé maker? Or do you simply try the recipe again, a different recipe or create your own, until you've made the soufflé you had envisioned? If I had gone by the first batch of garlic dill pickles my husband and I made with baby cucumbers from our garden, I'd be a lifetime failure as a pickle maker. They were so salty and soggy they were inedible. I dumped all six quarts down the garbage disposal and called our neighbors (I'd brought them a quart as a gift) and suggested they do the same. The next batch wasn't salty enough, yet was crispier. The third batch was nearly perfect, if a tad heavy on the garlic. Each batch brought us a step closer to the perfect pickle of our dreams. When I shared the salty batch with our neighbors, the six degrees of connection was put into action. From the neighbors, I received tips on growing our own dill, which I was in turn able to share with others. Who knows how many perfect pickles will be created down the road as a result?

When people want to protect you from hurt and failure, they are usually afraid to take risks and step out into the six degrees to create their own dreams. Your pursuing your dreams brings up their regrets and doubts. Their inner wounded child is talking, and their negativity isn't about you at all. You can be an inspiration, a conduit of the six degrees, for them. The key is to listen to the feelings being conveyed behind the words. Usually the feelings include some form of fear.

For example, your brother-in-law may warn you when he finds out you have decided to become part of a multi-level marketing company. You might simply ask why he feels that way. His response may be, "I tried three of those hoaxes, and all I got out of it was a big debt and a lot of wasted time and energy. What a crock! Don't do it!"

You may know someone (as I do) who has been very successful as a Shaklee representative or a Mary Kay consultant. You can use these concrete examples of how multi-level marketing can work, when the products and services are exceptional, and it's a good match for the person who is providing that product or service.

Know your PEG, listen before you respond, and respond instead of reacting.

TREAT OTHERS AS YOU WISH TO BE TREATED

When you know who you are and where you are going, applying the golden rule in your every day life will become second nature. You will listen before you respond. That's how you want to be treated. You will respond appropriately instead of reacting. That's how you want to be treated. You will give generously of your abundance with a sense of gratitude, not duty, knowing what you circulate comes back to you a hundred fold. You will be not only activating, but living within the six degrees of connection in the deepest and most meaningful part of you, thereby activating it in others.

> *One of the best feelings in the world is when someone tells you that you have been an answer to prayer. Isn't that incredible to think about? You, with all your complaints, messes, and shortcomings, can be an answer to somebody else's prayer. Wow.*
> —Moments for Myself, a calendar by Blessings Unlimited

> *The human heart has*
> *hidden treasure*
> *In secret kept,*
> *In silence sealed;*
> *The thoughts, the hopes,*
> *the dreams, the pleasure,*
> *Whose charms were*
> *broken if revealed.*
> —Charlotte Bronte

<u>Overview of Concept Five:</u>

- Share your dreams with positive people

- Turn to your WW circle for support and encouragement

- Prepare for change and possibly resistance from others as you create your dreams

- Write down your PEG: know it, use it, live it!

- Listen to fears and feelings behind other people's words

- Apply the golden rule in your daily life

CONCEPT *Six*

Overcoming Roadblocks

Mon. Small wash. We picked apples because the birds are spoiling them. Hail did a good job too. I can still get pies out of them but they won't keep. Got enough for three pies today.

—September 14, 1981

I use the term "perceived obstacle." A roadblock can look like a huge, insurmountable boulder in a dusty road. What to do with it? Climb over it? Can't roll it away—get some help to move it? Work your way around it? Take a different path?

Any or all of these options may be appropriate, depending on what that boulder represents to you. Your perceived obstacle could be an illness, or that of a family member. A death. It could be a financial challenge, a move, or even another opportunity which causes you to question the path of your dreams.

I've had perceived obstacles just like everyone else. Starting a business while my husband was the major breadwinner challenged my belief in myself as an independent and self-sufficient career woman. I was working from home much of the time when two of the three sons in our family from my husband's first marriage moved in with us within six months of each other, both at age sixteen. We've dealt with teenage pregnancy, arrests, marital discord and I've had plenty of my own personal issues and barriers to overcome. I'm not perfect. My family and friends aren't perfect, and we don't have perfect, orderly lives. I don't know anyone who does.

We do have six degrees of connection to our dreams, however.

While working through some of my challenges and launching my business, I took several different part time jobs. At one I met Karen. It was the first and only job I've ever been fired from. Karen shared with me the first Living the Dream story I wrote, and I made a new friend. She had teen daughters and we talked about the challenges and opportunities involved in raising teenagers. A challenge truly is an opportunity, if only we look at it that way. What does that boulder represent to you?

> *Do whatever comes your way to do as well as you can. Think as little as possible about yourself and as much as possible about other people and about things that are interesting. Put a good deal of thought into the happiness that you are able to give.*
> —Theodore Roosevelt

GIVE TO YOURSELF FIRST

Wise words from Mr. Roosevelt. There's one best way to give to others, and that is to give to yourself first. Good financial advisors say to pay yourself first. The same is true of your emotional bank account. None of us can share what we don't have to give. Replenish your well so you can water dreamers left and right, north and south, up and down! Take a solo retreat to a beautiful area (the coast, mountains, prairie, river) for a half day, an entire weekend if you can. Bring only inspirational reading material, your journal and a pen. Leave the computer, phone, TV and stereo behind. Pay attention to everything you see, hear, smell, touch. Everything will have meaning in it. Sleep well and deep. You will come back to your daily life completely rejuvenated.

IF I CAN'T, SOMEONE CAN

Is something really bothering you? So much so you can't stop thinking about it? Get yourself a can. Or a jar. Set the can aside for one specific purpose, to put your worries in, knowing if you can't deal with it, someone else can. The someone else could be your higher power (you can call it a God Can) or your WW circle. Write your worries down on a piece of paper. Fold the piece of paper and put it in the can. Make it symbolic, a ritual, knowing you no longer have to worry about that issue. Your IVIN will help you sort it out and your local WW circle will bring you right back to the six degrees to your dreams. You can forget about it for now. Whenever the worry resurfaces, remind yourself, "That is in the can!"

WHAT CAN I DO RIGHT NOW?

This is an alternate on the same theme. Let's say you wake up at 3:00 in the morning with a concern on your mind, something that won't let you sleep. Grab your journal and write down exactly what you can do about it right now. Chances are at 3:00 a.m. it will be nothing. But you can make a list of what you will do at 8:00 a.m. You just helped yourself get back to sleep, made a plan, and kicked the six degrees right back in place. Congratulations!

SET ASIDE WORRY TIME

This is yet another alternate on the same theme. Put a slot on your calendar every week for worrying, say, Friday afternoons from 2:00—4:00. Every time a concern or fear surfaces, write it on your calendar during that weekly time slot and say to yourself, "I'll worry about this then." You just unloaded your mind so your creativity can resurface. And, you'll probably find come 2:00 on Friday, whatever it was you were worrying about is no longer an issue. Either that, or there are other things on Friday afternoon you'd much rather do than worry!

What we feel, think, and do this moment influences both
our present and the future in ways we may never know.
Begin. Start right where you are. Consider your possibilities
and find inspiration…to add more meaning and zest to
your life.
—Alexandra Stoddard

<u>Overview of Concept Six:</u>

- No obstacles are insurmountable; they only appear that way
- Do whatever it takes to move through fear and worry

CONCLUSION

Life is a series of opportunities. When you tap into the six degrees of connection between everything, more and more opportunities will be presented to you, along with growth and learning experiences. Every encounter, each moment, is another opportunity to realize your dreams and help create the dreams of others.

This can feel like an overwhelming responsibility at times. Yet it doesn't have to be.

As we conclude our time together, for now, I'd like to share a prayer with you. You have probably heard it before. The words of this prayer have been attributed to different people; to my knowledge, noone knows for sure who wrote it. If you don't use the word God, simply substitute Life Force, Universal Energy, or whatever term works for you.

God, grant me the
SERENITY
to accept the things I cannot change,
COURAGE
to change the things I can,
and
WIDSOM
to know the difference.

It may be true none of us can change the world.

I thought I could change the world. It took me a hundred
years to figure out I can't change the world. I can only
change Bessie.
—Bessie Delany (written at age 104!)

CONCLUSION

Collectively, within just six degrees, we can make a difference by realizing our dreams and helping others realize theirs. In 1970, my grandmother regretted not going to Alaska. In 1971, she went to Alaska. It was one of the greatest adventures of her life.

Here's to your adventures, and your dreams. I'll see you at the pinnacle.

All Best Wishes, Laura Handke Jones

ACKNOWLEDGEMENTS

It is with deepest gratitude I acknowledge and thank Patty duToit, Judy Yriarte, Sally Shackelford, Patricia J. Hutchings, Cristy Bailey, Mary Meyer, Suzanne McKenna, Laura Roderick, Juliem Garland, Joni Riley, Leah Maka Grey, Rhonda Benton, Don Strike, Julie Dalke, Keli Kree, Dr. Steve Koc and the Heartbeat band for your contributions to M^6, the very first Wishweavers workshop and video and the first *How to Create a Wishweavers Experience* draft booklet. Thank you, Jenny Limbaugh, for the incredible song; thank you, Richard, Max, Steve, and Shawn Gritton of Catch a Wave Sound Studios for bringing your amazing talents to the recording. Thank you, AJ Talley, Lois Erickson and every woman ever involved in M^6! Patty, also, thank you for helping with Visualize, Journalize, Vocalize!

I've been blessed to work with some incredible clients and colleagues, whom I consider friends. Thank you for trusting me and each other with your precious wishes and dreams.

Thank you to Lee Jones, Dale Kennedy, Mary Meyer and Cheryl Gribskov, who served on the Wishweavers advisory board when my business was still just a wish. Lorraine Neff, thank you for the opportunities and generous guidance.

I'd like to thank my parents, brother, in-laws and extended family for always being there for me. Cara, thanks for setting up my first website for such a very good price—free!

Erik Estrada, thank you for reminding me dreams do come true, and thanks to Brian and Shawn Chrisagis, two more big dreamers.

I'm grateful for my incredible circle of creative and supportive friends—you know who you are. Betty, you've always been one of my biggest cheerleaders and I have deep respect and appreciation for you. June, thank you for your support, wisdom and inspiration during our weekly mini-Wishweaver phone check-ins. You've helped me stay motivated, on track and have provided me with alternative solutions and avenues I wouldn't have thought of on my own.

Rocky Bellew and Kathie Van Loh, I most likely would not have written this book without you. I'm profoundly grateful to you for sharing your amazing gifts with the written word, your motivation and your support. Robert Morris, formerly of the Institute of Children's Literature, you were a truly great writing teacher. Janelle Love and Michelle Cattanach, you may have no idea how much your support at SAIF Corporation meant to me. Writing and teaching that first business writing skills class is what really piqued my interest in training and facilitating. Elizabeth Lyon, one writing workshop with you turned my writing life around in the right direction. Art Bobrowitz, thank you for your always willing-to-help attitude; you're a true professional. Thank you, NanDei, Sasquia, Julie, Rocky, Ursula and Nancy for being willing to look at the very first draft of my very first manuscript and kindly tell me not only where it was bad but also where it was good. Thank you Dan, Lisa, June and Kara for helping me find the journal entries. Doug, thanks for being the first to ask for a ticket on the Oprah show.

Dr. Linda Taylor, thanks for the WHAT CAN I DO RIGHT NOW? exercise! Rev. Mary Manin Morrissey, thanks for the GOD CAN!

Thank you, Karen, Lori, Marie, Karl and the Novaks for trusting your Living the Dream stories with me even before I knew what I was doing. Kay Allenbaugh, thank you for assisting me with the permission form. Here's to chocolate! Sandie, your comments on the first booklet were helpful as I was drafting these chapters. Amy, I appreciate your friendship and web diva skills.

Joan Bramsch, your inspiration and input were invaluable as I was preparing to take the big leap into the unknown. You guided me over the edge when I didn't realize I could fly. Thank you for the wonderful Personal Expansion Goal (PEG) suggestion. You were right, of course.

Thank you to successful, best-selling authors Gail Blanke, Laura Day, Malcolm Gladwell, and Barbara Stanny (and Oriana.) Your books helped me first; then you helped me personally when I called on you for assistance. I strive to emulate your integrity and character. I'm forever grateful to Stephanie Tade, Stephanie Peterson, Joshua Bagby, Geronimo Tagatac, and my talented cousin, Kathryn Penniston. Carol White—I don't know what else to say except YOU ROCK! Thanks also to the great iUniverse staff.

Naima, do you remember that day, sitting on the carpet, leaning against the wall, at Oprah's first Live Your Best Life conference in San Francisco? You gave me the idea to combine Grandma's story with the book I already had brewing. You are an amazing woman. Strappy shoes and gold ankle bracelets are yours!

Marcia Wieder, America's Dream Coach, you are an inspiration to me.

Especially, thank you, Jeff, my husband, beloved partner and best friend. With you I've learned the true meaning of the word commitment, when to make sacrifices and why, how great it is to just laugh and have fun and what intimacy is truly about. You are a person of great honor and I honor you.

RESOURCE DIRECTORY

See www.wishweavers.com for a complete and regularly updated recommended reading list.

If you have a dream, Wishweavers has already done 90% of the work for you! Check out our lively discussion forum to receive and share resources with people from all over the world—it's absolutely free! Sign up for free weekly WW tips!

Are you ready? A Wishweavers Experience will:

- Help you discover, clarify, define and affirm your dreams, goals and wishes

- Share resources, information, contacts and strategies

- Teach through your active participation in one-on-one exchanges and small groups

- Furnish the tools to create dreams at home, at school, or in the workplace

- Present effective strategies through collective brainstorming and action

- Place emphasis on creative thinking with sold steps for follow through

Wishweavers forums provide the additional knowledge you have been seeking. They are affordable, accessible and inspirational. You will leave the experience with your personal treasure map, knowing the steps to take to achieve your dream; assured of ongoing support and motivation.

It's never too late to start on the path to your dreams, your deepest wishes, your heartfelt desires. Contact us today.

www.wishweavers.com
laura@wishweavers.com
503.581.2134

Dream it…Believe it…Achieve it…

Wishweavers **Services:**

Wishweavers workshops
Individual sessions
Teleconferences
Limited time focus groups
Speaking engagements
Business and educational forums
Writing workshops
Creative event facilitation

Wishweavers is a professional connecting service.
Available **Resources** include but are not limited to:

Published writers
Editors
Publishers
Sound studios
Weight management and wellness consultants
Counselors
Coaches
Naturopathic and acupunctural medicine
Homeopathic healing
Dream interpretation
Time and memory management
Parent coaching

If you need a resource, chances are Wishweavers can find it!

Helping people who are passionate about realizing their dreams,
and organizations wishing to align with their creative potential...

It's not because things are difficult that we dare not, it's
because we dare not that things are difficult.
—Seneca

SIX DEGREES TO YOUR DREAMS...

A Tribute to Grandma Handke
Sept. 1, 1999

This angel on earth was an extraordinary woman, someone my brother, Jason, and I were blessed to call "Grandma." We heard the stories many times of how she worked her way through college for her board and room (that's how she worded it, not room and board) sending money to help out her younger sister, Martha, in foster care when she could. Their parents both died very young. To think Grandma went to college and earned her degree in 1930, a young woman with no support other than herself in that time period, is mind boggling to me now. When I was younger, I didn't fully understand what it must have been like for her, when she would talk about working for her board and room, some of the people she lived with during those years, about the women friends she met in college. How she worried so about Martha. Norma Handke was a woman of strength, perseverance and faith. She taught in a small country school for one year, until she met and married our grandfather, Lee Handke, in 1932.

It was lonely for her on the farm at first. She said it took a long time for her to adjust to the rolling prairies by Raymond, South Dakota, she eventually grew to love and call home. All the trees they planted surely helped. And gardening, which was one of Grandma's abiding, constant loves. She even made the *Watertown Public Opinion* newspaper on July 24, 1979! With a big color photo of Norma Handke in her "Informal Gardens," as the caption read. Trillium was one of her particular favorites, and she dearly loved iris. She loved all God's foliage, and was quite the weeder, a trait her granddaughter didn't inherit!

And baseball. Need I say more? Oh…yes. Two words. "Minnesota Twins."

Grandma was the proverbial grandmother in many way—in an apron, in the kitchen, baking cookies. I saw her as many times wearing an apron as not. And there was always candy in the candy dish. Butterscotch, peppermints, and sometimes the softer chewier stuff. Her "handiwork" is some of the best I've seen. Crocheting, especially. She loved to have something to keep her hands busy while she was watching…you got it, baseball on TV.

Grandma was an avid reader and passed along (like Grandpa) her thirst for learning to her two sons—Jason's and my father, Donald, and our Uncle Glenn. She loved birds. Her expansive vocabulary about the feathered creatures was rivaled, probably, only by her knowledge of plant life. She also loved cats, and sometimes that was a source of stress for her—birds and cats…well, you know.

Grandma Handke was a woman of strong opinions. A couple I disagreed with (silently) and still do. The opinions I most remember and paid attention to were to stop biting my fingernails, and to stand up straight, pay attention to my posture!

When I think of Grandma, I recall how we used to trek into the trees surrounding the back yard until we got to our "special" picnic place. We would have made lemonade and a lunch, or just something sweet to snack on, and brought it with us. I can picture her bending under the trees, pushing aside the branches, until we got to that one place that was "ours." When she first introduced me to tea, I preferred green tea. So she made green tea when I came over. I remember having tea parties with her and Grandpa in their travel trailer outside. I'm not sure why we went to the trailer instead of sitting at the kitchen table in the house. It must have seemed more special, like going to a restaurant. I remember stopping by when I was horseback riding, and Princess or Blondie would wait outside while I chatted with Grandma.

I loved singing with Grandma in church, her lovely soprano harmonizing with my alto. She loved that, too. About three years ago I called, and coaxed her into singing "Amazing Grace" with me over the phone. She started crying before we were done with the song.

Grandma and I were always close, but I got to know her better when I went to college, then moved away from South Dakota. The phone calls and letters we exchanged over the years gave me insight into her as a woman, a person, and a child of God, I'd never known before. She became my friend.

Grandma was a wonderful letter writer. Her words were heartfelt and her letters were always descriptive and "newsy," even later on when she felt she had nothing to write about. Her hand-written script was lovely, and she always told me to work on my penmanship when I was younger. I ended up using a typewriter and later, computer! Grandma always wrote on lovely stationery, usually with the envelope garnished by stamps of a foundation she was supporting. National Geographic, Readers Digest…oh, Grandma subscribed to many different things.

Grandma embraced the three sons in our family from Jeff's first marriage. She called Derek, Cameron, and Chad her grandchildren. She asked about them constantly before she started to lose her memory. The boys got to meet her before she started to slip away. They all remember her. I have a picture of the three of them with Grandma, which speaks more than words could ever say.

Grandma's faith in God was a sustaining force for her. She passed that faith on to me at every opportunity. In one photograph from my high school church confirmation, Grandma is standing before me just after we released each other from a huge hug. It's impossible to say which one of our smiles is bigger. The joy in that fading picture still radiates from my photo album page. The card she gave me that day speaks of the pride and happiness she felt, that her wish for me was God's presence, love, and joy. For always.

And now that is my wish for her, a wish I know is already granted. As much as I will miss her, I'm happy, grateful, and blessed to know Norma Amelia Hahn Handke, or—as I've always called her—Grandma Handke, is with God, the angels, and…finally…her beloved husband again. Those of us she left behind have a guardian angel while we're still here on earth. That is the biggest blessing I could ever hope to have. I love you, Grandma. We all do.

978-0-595-36193-9
0-595-36193-5

Printed in the United States
34011LVS00006B/241-474